Lee Mansion
⎯⎯⎯☆ NATIONAL MEMORIAL
VIRGINIA

by Murray H. Nelligan

NATIONAL PARK SERVICE HISTORICAL HANDBOOK SERIES No. 6
WASHINGTON, D. C., 1953

UNITED STATES DEPARTMENT OF THE INTERIOR
Douglas McKay, *Secretary*

NATIONAL PARK SERVICE
Conrad L. Wirth, *Director*

Lee Mansion

National Memorial – Virginia

By Murray H. Nelligan

All rights reserved, which include the right to reproduce this book or portions thereof in any form except provided by U.S Copyright Laws.

Digital Scanning and Publishing is a leader in the electronic republication of historical books and documents. We publish many of our titles as eBooks, paperback and hardcover editions. DSI is committed to bringing many traditional and well-known books back to life, retaining the look and feel of the original work.

Trade Paperback ISBN: 978-1-58218-886-7

© 2017 DSI Digital Reproduction

First DSI Printing: 2017
Published by Digital Scanning, Inc. Scituate, MA 02066.
781-545-2100 www,digitalscanning.com

Contents

	Page
History of Arlington to 1861	1
Arlington from 1861 to 1865	24
Arlington from 1865 to the Present	26
Guide to the House and Grounds	28
Visitor Service and Facilities	46
Administration	47

> The National Park System, of which Lee Mansion is a part, is dedicated to the conservation of America's scenic, scientific, and historic heritage for the benefit and enjoyment of the people.

General Robert E. Lee in 1865. From the original photograph by Mathew Brady in the National Archives.

Ever since it was built more than a century ago, the Lee Mansion has dominated the scene across the river from the National Capital. An outstanding example of a Greek Revival building of the early nineteenth century, its dignity and strength, simplicity and steady grace, now make it a most appropriate national memorial to one of America's greatest men, Robert E. Lee.

Built by his father-in-law, George Washington Parke Custis, the adopted son of General Washington, the mansion was for many years a principal repository of the George Washington tradition. As such, it greatly influenced Robert E. Lee when the building was his home. Like him, it experienced the vicissitudes of war and came to be associated with his fame. Now it is maintained by the Nation in his honor, and in the years to come will serve as a constant reminder of his nobility and greatness.

Many years have passed since General Lee lived in the home at Arlington. But so real are the memories evoked by its historic atmosphere, it seems little more than yesterday that he left it for the last time. A visit to the Lee Mansion gives a deeper, more personal understanding of the life and worth of the man to whose memory it is now dedicated.

History of Arlington to 1861

ANCESTRY OF GEORGE WASHINGTON PARKE CUSTIS. George Washington Parke Custis was born April 30, 1781. His mother was Eleanor (Calvert) Custis, a granddaughter of the sixth Lord Baltimore; his father, John Parke Custis, the only son of Martha Washington by her first marriage. John Parke Custis grew to manhood at Mount Vernon, married Eleanor Calvert in 1774, and died of camp fever in 1781 while serving as aide to General Washington at Yorktown. His death left four children fatherless, so the two youngest, George Washington Parke Custis and his sister Eleanor, were adopted by the Washingtons and taken to Mount Vernon to be raised as their own.

HIS EARLY LIFE AT MOUNT VERNON.   Only 6 months old when he was taken to live at Mount Vernon, it was a remarkable experience for a boy as sensitive and gifted as young Custis to grow up on terms of intimacy with General Washington, whose affection the fatherless lad reciprocated with the deepest love and respect. As far as public duties would allow, the General supervised the training and education of the boy, who acquired from him the interests and ideals which established the pattern of his life. "It is really an enjoyment to be here to witness the tranquil happiness that reigns throughout the house," wrote a guest at Mount Vernon in 1799, "except when now and then a little bustle is occasioned by the young Squire Custis when he returns from hunting, bringing in a 'valiant deer', as he terms it, that Grandpa and the Colonel will devour: nice venison I assure you."

GEORGE WASHINGTON PARKE CUSTIS MOVES TO ARLINGTON.   Custis was 19 when the General died in 1799. Mrs. Washington did not long survive her husband, and when she died, early in 1802, Custis moved to "Mount Washington," as he first called the Arlington estate. This was a tract of 1,100 acres that Custis' father had bought in 1778 with the intention of establishing a family seat convenient to Mount Vernon, but in 1802 the only tangible remains of his brief ownership were the flourishing willows he had planted along the Potomac.

"ARLINGTON HOUSE" BEGUN.   When Custis moved into a cottage built by the former owners of the property, Arlington consisted mostly of woodland and virgin oak forests, with a few cleared fields near the river. His first concern was to get the fields under cultivation, using for the purpose the mules and farm equipment he had purchased at the sales held that year at Mount Vernon to settle the legacies of the several Washington heirs. Equally urgent was the need to build a house worthy of the furnishings and mementoes which he had inherited or bought at the Mount Vernon sales, some of which were deteriorating badly in their temporary quarters. To this end, he seems to have obtained building plans from George Hadfield, a gifted young architect, who had come from England in 1795 to take charge of the construction of the Capitol.

Influenced by the contemporary vogue for classical architecture, Custis wanted his house to be in the new style, and the architect's finished design was a simplified Greek Doric portico balanced by extended wings, the whole of such sturdiness as to show to advantage when viewed from across the river. Since ornamentation would be lost at such a distance, the architect largely dispensed with it, relying on good proportions to give beauty to his creation. Rooms would be large and have high ceilings and tall windows, and their severely plain walls would be perfect for displaying the many portraits Custis possessed. Having the rooms open into each other would give extensive vistas, framed by pleasing semicircular arches.

Coat of arms of the Custis Family.

George Washington Parke Custis. From a miniature made at Mount Vernon in 1799.

Though clay for bricks and choice timber were at hand on his estate, Custis lacked the money necessary to build his house all at once. Therefore he followed the common practice of building the wings first, and the main section later. The north wing was built soon after Custis came to Arlington, and was evidently intended to be one great banquet room. By 1804, the south wing was completed, containing an office and a large room for entertaining. In that year Custis married Mary Lee Fitzhugh. To provide living quarters for himself and his bride he had the north wing partitioned into three small rooms. With a kitchen and laundry in the basement, the young couple had the essentials of living at "Arlington House," as Custis named his new home, after the old family seat on the Eastern Shore. At this point, work seems to have been stopped. A visitor reported in 1811, "I was struck, on entering the grounds of Mr. Custis, at Arlington, . . . with several of the most picturesque views. This seat is on a superb mount, and his buildings are begun in a stile of superior taste and elegance."

ARLINGTON AND THE DEVELOPMENT OF AMERICAN AGRICULTURE. While building his house, Custis inaugurated an annual fair designed to improve agricultural practices in general, and particularly the breeding of fine-wooled sheep. Beginning in 1803, Custis invited the local gentry each spring to exhibit their best sheep and homespun cloth at Arlington Spring, near the edge of the river. After prizes had been awarded, the fair would close with patriotic speeches and a great dinner under the tent which had been used by Washington during the Revolution.

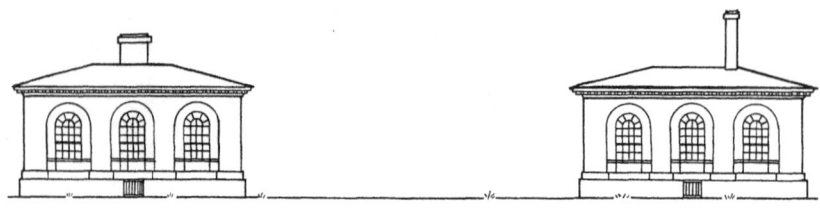

"ARLINGTON HOUSE," AS IT APPEARED FROM ABOUT 1804-1816

By breeding the native stock on his farms with the imported stock he had acquired from Mount Vernon, Custis himself developed a hardy race of fine-wooled sheep, known as the "Arlington Improved." Because the wool of this breed could be woven into finer cloth than hitherto possible, the Arlington sheep were widely diffused throughout the country. Custis also sought to correct the primitive agricultural methods which had already caused much land in his State to be abandoned because of soil erosion. He advocated the establishment of a National Board of Agriculture with functions like those of the Department of Agriculture today, and he offered one of his outlying properties for use as an experimental breeding station. So popular was the Arlington Sheepshearing, as it was commonly called, that the idea was quickly adopted elsewhere. Though economic conditions forced Custis to discontinue the event after 1812, it was one of the primary sources of the great program of agricultural improvement in effect today.

BIRTH OF MARY ANNE RANDOLPH CUSTIS. Mary Anne Randolph Custis, born in 1808, was the only one of the four Custis children to survive the first year of infancy. Upon her the parents centered their affections and hopes. The mother's natural piety and devotion to her family were deepened by the loss of her other children, while the father's warm and generous nature was such that in later years she could not recall ever having received an unkind word from him.

CUSTIS AND THE WAR OF 1812. During the War of 1812, the British blockade of the Chesapeake deprived Custis of much of the income from his other estates, so it is doubtful if any building was done at Arlington at this time. Convinced that Napoleon threatened the liberties of mankind more than England, Custis strongly opposed the war. For this reason he was chosen to deliver the funeral oration for General Lingan, a veteran of the Revolution who was murdered by the same Baltimore mob which almost killed Robert E. Lee's father, "Light-Horse Harry" Lee. Nevertheless, Custis followed the example set by George Washington during the American Revolution by forbidding the managers of his plantations to furnish supplies to the British; and when British troops approached the National Capital in 1814, Custis fought in the ranks at the battle of Bladensburg.

Arlington Spring, scene of the famous "Sheepshearings."

"ARLINGTON HOUSE" COMPLETED. After the war, Custis resumed work on his house, and the large center section and great portico appear to have been finished by 1817. "A house that any one might see with half an eye," as Robert E. Lee later described it, could not fail to attract attention, and "Custis' Folly" is first mentioned by a traveler in 1818. Although the interior was never completed as planned and the rear was left unstuccoed, "Arlington House" was soon considered one of the handsomest residences about Washington. One early writer describes it as "a noble-looking place, having a portico of stately white columns, which, as the mansion stands high, with a back ground of dark woods, forms a beautiful object in the landscape."

THE MEMORY OF GEORGE WASHINGTON KEPT ALIVE AT ARLINGTON. "Arlington House" now became the successor of Mount Vernon as the "Washington Treasury," as Custis termed it. His collection of Washington relics was the largest in existence, and it filled the halls and rooms of the mansion. The owner of these relics welcomed all who wished to view them, and he never tired of entertaining his guests with tales of his early years at Mount Vernon. Many distinguished men visited Arlington at one time or other—Sam Houston, Daniel Webster, and Andrew Jackson, to name a few. One of the most notable was General Lafayette, who twice was a guest there when he toured the United States in 1824 and 1825. Custis spent much time with the venerable marquis, and used the wealth of reminiscenses he gained from the old soldier to write the delightful *Conversations With Lafayette,* which was published in a local newspaper in 1825. Encouraged by their favorable reception, he then began his own *Recollections and Private Memoirs of Washington,* which proved equally popular and were widely reprinted in the newspapers of the period.

Even more successful were the dramas Custis wrote at this time, based on heroic episodes in the Nation's past or on inspiring contemporary achievements. *The Indian Prophecy* used an incident in Washington's early life as its theme and established a vogue for Indian plays which lasted over 50 years; while the *Rail Road* was the first one written on that subject in America. Others dramatized such events as the battle of Baltimore and the launching of a new warship. For 10 years his dramatic pieces were staged from Boston to Charleston and did much to develop a distinctive American drama.

A man of culture, Custis used all of his abilities to perpetuate the memory of Washington. He erected the first monument on the Presi-

An early view of "Arlington House." From an engraving made about 1845.

The tents used by General Washington during the American Revolution were cherished relics at Arlington.

dent's birthplace in 1815, wrote poems to celebrate his greatness, and painted unskilled, but colorful battle pictures in which the great General was the central figure. An accomplished orator, he was tireless in advocating the principles of freedom for which Washington had fought, and planned to do with his slaves as his foster father had done—free them after they had been prepared to shift for themselves. Although he never held an elective office, his influence was considerable and for the good.

HOME LIFE AT ARLINGTON. An equal source of inspiration at "Arlington House" was the religious atmosphere of its home life. Mrs. Custis was a devout Episcopalian, noted for her simplicity and piety. It was she who influenced Robert E. Lee's Sunday school teacher, Bishop William Meade, to enter the ministry. Diligent where her husband was inclined to be easy-going, Mrs. Custis was one with him in making Arlington free from ostentation.

Kept unspoiled by her parents' example, Mary Custis was given the education deemed necessary for a young lady of her position, and as soon as she was old enough herself taught the children of nearby families and family servants. Though an only child, she never lacked companionship, for usually the house overflowed with relatives and their children. The Custises, too, often went visiting, especially to "Ravensworth," formerly the home of Mrs. Custis' father and now owned by her only brother. Here Mary must have played as a child with Robert E. Lee, for he and his mother were also related to the Fitzhughs and often visited at their estate. No doubt the Lees were familiar with Arlington as well, for the family tradition is that Robert was a favorite with the Custises from boyhood. He and Mary Custis are said to have planted some of the trees in the vicinity of the house when they were young.

POCAHONTAS;

OR,

THE SETTLERS OF VIRGINIA,

A NATIONAL DRAMA,

IN THREE ACTS.

Performed at the Walnut Street Theatre, Philadelphia, twelve nights, with great success.

WRITTEN BY

GEORGE WASHINGTON CUSTIS, ESQ.

Of Arlington House. Author of the Rail Road, Pawnee Chief, &c. &c.

PHILADELPHIA EDITION.
C. ALEXANDER, PR.

1830.

Title page of the 1830 edition of Custis' most popular play.

MARRIAGE OF MARY CUSTIS AND ROBERT E. LEE. Childhood friendship turned to love by the time Lee graduated from West Point and was assigned to duty in the Corps of Engineers. Whenever possible he was at Arlington courting Mary Custis, and in the summer of 1830 they became engaged.

The evening of the wedding, June 30, 1831, was one of steady rain, but nothing could affect the warmth and happiness inside the friendly portals of Arlington. The ceremony was formal and elaborate as befitted the union of two of the most prominent families of Virginia; and the soft candlelight shining on the happy couple, surrounded by pretty bridesmaids and uniformed groomsmen, made a picture never to be forgotten by those who saw it.

THE LEES AT FORT MONROE, 1831 TO 1834. Wedding trips not being customary at that time, the young married couple stayed at Arlington until it was time for them to go to Fort Monroe where Lee was stationed. At Christmas they returned home, and, because of the bad weather, Mrs. Lee remained there till spring. Furniture and choice provisions from the Custis farms helped to make the Lee's quarters at the fort more home-

George Washington Parke Custis. Engraved from the portrait by Gilbert Stuart made about 1825.

Lieutenant and Mrs. Robert E. Lee in 1838. From the portraits by William E. West. U. S. Army Signal Corps photographs.

like, while Mrs. Custis' frequent letters lessened her daughter's homesickness, as did the whimsical, chatty ones her father wrote regularly to his "Dr Son & Daughter." In September of 1832, their first child was born there, a son named George Washington Custis Lee, after his grandfather. Christmas that year at Arlington was especially happy because of the new baby (known familiarly as "Custis" Lee), and because Lee was unexpectedly able to be there. The following year passed much the same way.

LEE ON DUTY AT WASHINGTON, 1834 TO 1837. In the autumn of 1834, Lee was transferred to Washington and with his family made his home at Arlington. Sometimes his work kept him away overnight, but usually each morning and afternoon he was to be seen riding between his office and home. Lee disliked the office work which kept him in the city until the middle of 1837, but life at Arlington was most pleasant. Mrs. Lee's parents idolized their little grandson, and for them Lee felt a growing respect and affection. Custis was the nearest link to the first President, and associating with him and living in the presence of so many of the General's personal belongings made Washington very close and real to the young engineer, an example and influence that steadily entered his soul.

Lee fitted easily into the quiet way of life at Arlington. Mrs. Lee and her mother cared little for formal social affairs, preferring to be out of doors gardening or riding about the estate when not entertaining visitors. Mr. Custis was usually busy with his farm, and since he liked to hunt, he might often be seen walking or riding about the estate with his gun and dogs; evenings he spent with his family by the hearth, or retired to his study to work on his literary efforts. Each morning and evening the family and servants gathered for prayers, and grace was said before each meal. On Sundays the family usually drove into Alexandria to church, or held services at home if the roads were bad. Mrs. Lee, like her father, was an amateur artist, an interest shared by her husband who also occasionally assisted Mr. Custis in his business affairs or put his engineering experience to use in making improvements.

Troubles there were, of course. Lee was away on a mission to Ohio and Michigan when his second child, a daughter whom they named Mary, was born in the summer of 1835. When he returned, he found his wife so seriously ill that she was unable to walk for months. This was the first of a series of illnesses which were to make her an invalid much of her life.

Though this experience saddened Lee at the time, it made his home the more dear to him. It was about this time that he wrote to a friend: "The Country looks very sweet now, and the hill at Arlington covered with verdure, and perfumed by the blossoms of the trees, the flowers of the Garden. Honey-Suckles, yellow Jasmine, &c. is more to my taste than at any other season of the year. But the brightest flower there blooming is my daughter . . . [I] hurry home to her every day."

THE LEES AT ST. LOUIS, 1838 TO 1839. In 1837 another son was born, and although Lee had received orders to report to St. Louis he was able to remain at Arlington until he was assured the mother and baby were doing well. Christmas he was home again, remaining there till spring so Mrs. Lee and the two boys could return with him to St. Louis. Little Mary stayed behind with her grandparents, which may have compensated them somewhat for the absence of her parents the following Christmas.

Now a captain, Lee brought his family home in the spring of 1839 for Mrs. Lee to await the arrival of their fourth child, though he could

View from Arlington about 1837. From the original lithograph in the New York Public Library.

not remain for the event. Early in July, he heard a new daughter had joined the family circle, but not until Christmas did he get to see her.

An incident which probably occurred that winter illustrates the seriousness with which Lee viewed his family responsibilities. He and 8-year-old Custis had gone for a walk one snowy day, the boy following behind while his father broke the way. Preoccupied with ploughing through the deep snow, the father failed to look behind for some time, and when he did, saw that his little son was setting his feet carefully in the tracks his father had made, while imitating his every movement. "When I saw this," Lee related afterwards, "I said to myself, 'It behooves me to walk very straight, when the little fellow is already following in my tracks'."

LEE AT FORT HAMILTON, N. Y., 1841 TO 1846. Lee did not return to St. Louis until the summer of 1840, and then only to finish up his work and return home. There his fifth child, a girl, was born the following February. Soon after, Lee was sent to Fort Hamilton, N. Y., where he remained on duty until 1846. During these years it was customary for his family to be with him at New York during the summer and fall months and at Arlington the rest of the year, where Lee usually passed the winter. Two more children, a boy and a girl, were born in these years. Telling a friend about the arrival of the boy, Lee wrote: "About a month ago a young Robert E. Lee made his appearance at Arlington, much to the surprise and admiration of his brothers and sisters. He has a fine long nose like his father, but no whiskers."

WAR WITH MEXICO, 1846 TO 1848. Because war with Mexico seemed imminent when Lee went back to Fort Hamilton in the spring of 1846, Mrs. Lee and the children remained at Arlington. Hostilities began in May, and in August Lee was ordered to report for service in Mexico. Returning home, he spent a few days at Arlington arranging his affairs, then said goodbye to his family. Twenty-two months passed before he saw it again, months of anxiety for those waiting at home, relieved only by his long and frequent letters, such as the one he wrote to his two eldest sons the day before Christmas, 1846: "I hope good Santa Claus will fill my Rob's stocking to-night: that Mildred's, Agnes's, and Anna's may break down with good things. I do not know what he may have for you and Mary, but if he only leaves for you one half of what I wish, you will want for nothing!"

The war ended early in 1848, and seeing many of the returning volunteers enjoy Mr. Custis' hospitality at Arlington Spring must have made the Lees more impatient for the return of their own hero. When Lee finally arrived in Washington he missed the carriage sent for him, and so procured a horse to ride home. None of those anxiously watching for a glimpse of the carriage noticed the lone horseman ascending the hill, and not till "Spec," Lee's dog, rushed out joyfully barking did they realize their soldier was home. Great was the excitement as he greeted

Robert E. Lee in civilian dress, about 1850.

them in the hall, and his mistaking a friend's little boy for his own added to the hilarity. "Here I am again, my dear Smith," Lee wrote to his brother the next day, "perfectly surrounded by Mary and her precious children, who seem to devote themselves to staring at the furrows in my face and the white hairs in my head . . . I find them too much grown, and all well, and I have much cause for thankfulness and gratitude to that good God who has once more united us."

THE LEES AT ARLINGTON, 1848 TO 1849. The summer of 1848 was a happy one at Arlington, for Lee was on duty in Washington and was promoted to brevet colonel, so that hereafter he would be titled "Colonel Lee." Toward the end of the year he was assigned to supervise the construction of a new fort in Baltimore, but soon after officially taking over the project, he returned to Arlington. This was the winter that a guest at Arlington observed Lee's face in quiet repose as he read to his family assembled about the table one night, and thought to herself: "You certainly look more like a great man than any one I have ever seen."

Mrs. Lee and her mother made an equally favorable impression on a lady who visited Arlington the next spring. "We had tea in the Washington teacups, and Mrs. Lee took me into the tangled neglected gardens, full of rose-buds, and allowed me to pick my fill of the sweet dainty Bon Silene variety, which she told me blossomed all winter. What a view that was! . . . Mrs. Lee had the face of a genius: a wealth of dark hair, carelessly put up, gave her fine head the air of one of Romney's portraits. She was most lovely and sympathetic. Her mother, Mrs. Custis, was a woman full of character."

THE LEES AT BALTIMORE, 1849 TO 1852. Lee was home for a short time during the summer of 1849 to recuperate from a touch of fever, and in the autumn his family joined him at Baltimore. There they lived through 1851, coming home for Christmas and occasional visits. Seldom was the family together, however, for their eldest son, Custis, entered West Point in 1850, and usually some of the children were at Arlington with their grandparents.

Mrs. Custis kept the absent ones informed as to what was going on at Arlington. "Your Grandfather is seized with a spirit of improvement lately," she wrote to the lad at West Point in 1851. "He is making new steps to the Portico (the old ones having so decayed as to be unsafe) and intends paving it with octagon brick tiles which are now being burned in the vast brick kilns in Washington." Later, she reported that the steps were finished and the portico floor about to be laid.

Though 70 and often unwell, Mr. Custis' activity seldom flagged. A polished and effective speaker, with a gift for being able to enter into the spirit of an occasion, he was well-liked for his personal charm and unassuming manner. He was fond of children, and a great favorite with the young Lees. Conscious of his advancing years, Custis increased the output of his *Recollections of Washington,* that his personal knowledge of the General might not be lost. In this he was encouraged by the Lees, who also approved his renewed interest in scientific agriculture. While strongly advocating the establishment of a department of agriculture in the National Government, Custis applied the latest methods of fertilizing and cultivation to his own farms so that the land inherited by his grandchildren would be fertile, rather than worn-out like that of so much of his native State.

A view of "Arlington House" made in 1853 by the historian-artist Benson J. Lossing. From the original water color in the Lee Mansion.

Christmas in 1851 was typical of the many happy ones celebrated at Arlington, and, telling his son at West Point about it, Lee wrote: "[We] found your grandfather at the Washington depot, Daniel and the old carriage and horses, and young Daniel on the colt Mildred. Your mother, grandfather, Mary Eliza, the little people, and the baggage, I thought load enough for the carriage, so Rooney and I took our feet in our hands and walked over. . . . The snow impeded the carriage as well as us, and we reached here shortly after it. The children were delighted at getting back, and passed the evening in devising pleasure for the morrow. They were in upon us before day on Christmas morning, to overhaul their stockings. . . . I need not describe to you our amusements, you have witnessed them so often; nor the turkey, cold ham, plum-pudding, mince pies, etc., at dinner." "Rooney" was the Lee's second boy, William Henry Fitzhugh.

George Washington Parke Custis in his old age. From the photograph by Mathew Brady in the collection of Frederick H. Meserve, New York.

THE LEES AT WEST POINT, 1852 TO 1855; DEATH OF MRS. CUSTIS. Lee took command of West Point in September 1852, where he was shortly joined by his family. Mrs. Custis had been well when they left, so the telegram which came in April telling of her critical illness was entirely unexpected. Mrs. Lee started for home at once, but on arrival found her beloved mother dead and her father prostrated by his loss. She at once took charge of the household and herself conducted the morning worship which had been forgotten in the sorrow and confusion. After breakfast she selected a spot for her mother's grave among the trees a short distance from the house. For years, Lee had called Mrs. Custis "Mother," and his grief at her death was almost as great as Mrs. Lee's. By now the religious convictions instilled in him by his mother had been matured by his own experiences and the example of those at Arlington, and soon after his return from West Point at the end of the term, he and two of his daughters were confirmed at Christ Church, Alexandria.

Hoping to divert Mr. Custis, the Lees took him back with them to West Point. But not even a trip to Niagara Falls with his son-in-law could keep him from worrying about his beloved Arlington, and he soon returned home. To ease his loneliness, the Lees came home on brief visits in the spring and summer of 1854 and were also there for Christmas.

LEE IN TEXAS, 1855 TO 1857.   Early in 1855, Lee was assigned to a cavalry regiment being organized for service on the frontier. Before leaving for his new station he made arrangements to have the large unfinished room off the main hall, at Arlington, made into a drawing room and to have a hot-air furnace installed to heat the house. The "Big Room," as it was called, when finished was very handsome with its marble mantelpieces and crystal chandelier, and Mrs. Lee and the girls were proud of its appearance when they showed it to Lee on his return for the holidays.

Much of his leave was given over to straightening out the finances of Mr. Custis' other farms, for the old gentleman was now 75 and, though active in improving his lands and crops, needed the assistance of his son-in-law in managing his business affairs. Lee returned to Texas in February 1856, and was unable to be home for Christmas that year. His loneliness is apparent in the letter he wrote to Mrs. Lee: "The time is approaching when I trust many of you will be assembled around the family hearth at dear Arlington, to celebrate another Christmas. Though absent, my heart will be in the midst of you, & I shall enjoy in imagination & memory, all that is going on. May nothing occur to mar or cloud the family fireside, & may each be able to look back with pride & pleasure at their deeds of the past year, & with confidence & hope to that in prospect. I can do nothing but hope & pray for you all."

DEATH OF MR. CUSTIS.   Life at Arlington and for the father far away in Texas flowed on quietly during 1857. Although badly crippled by rheumatism, Mrs. Lee was able to manage the household and spend much time in her garden, while her father occupied himself as usual. But in the fall a telegram came to Lee, telling him of Mr. Custis' death on October 10th. Letters from the family told him more of the sad event: how Mr. Custis had been ill of pneumonia only 4 days, how he had

Mrs. Robert E. Lee. This engraving was probably made from a photograph taken sometime after 1865.

steadily failed, and how on the last day, after embracing his weeping daughter and grandchildren and asking to be remembered to his son-in-law, had passed away while his rector said the prayers for the dying. His last wish had been to be buried by the side of his wife, and to that spot his coffin had been borne by the family servants, followed by the Lees and a host of relatives and friends.

LEE BECOMES MASTER OF ARLINGTON.   It was a saddened household to which Lee returned as soon as he could, made more so because Mrs. Lee's illness had progressed to where she was almost incapable of getting about the house. He found it necessary to take an extended leave in order to take on the management of Mr. Custis' properties and, as his executor, to carry out the terms of his will. This provided that after outstanding debts had been paid and legacies given each of the Lee girls, the farms were to go to the boys, although Mrs. Lee would have possession of Arlington until her death, after which it would pass to Custis Lee. All the slaves were to be freed within 5 years.

A large debt had to be paid off before anything else could be done, and Lee applied himself to making the farms as productive as possible by putting more land under cultivation and planting larger crops. For a time, it seemed that it would be impossible for him ever to discharge his obligations satisfactorily, but he could still hide his discouragement from his children, as when in the autumn of 1858 he came upon one of his daughters saying a tearful goodbye to a friend, and said cheerfully to the weeping girls: "No tears at Arlington, no tears." Fortunately, by the summer of 1859 he could see some improvement in the situation, although much remained to be done.

JOHN BROWN'S RAID AND THE IMPENDING CRISIS. One morning in October 1859, a young lieutenant, J. E. B. Stuart, who had been a guest at Arlington several times, came with orders for Lee to report at once to the Secretary of War. There he learned of John Brown's raid on Harpers Ferry and was directed to take command of the forces being sent to quell the uprising. This was soon accomplished, and in a short while Lee was home again.

Affairs at Arlington were so encouraging that autumn, that Lee expected soon to rejoin his regiment in Texas. Therefore, he arranged to have his son, Custis, who was now in the Corps of Engineers, transferred to Washington where he could supervise the estate. Unlike many army officers, Lee had never been away long from his native State, and his months of hard work at Arlington had given him a sympathetic understanding of the problems faced by his kinsmen and fellow-planters and reaffirmed his belief that his first loyalty was to Virginia.

These were his views when he went to Texas in February 1860, and they remained unchanged as the discord between the North and South grew more intense. Uneasily, he observed the recklessness of the extremists on both sides, hoping always that the Union he loved would be preserved. Texas seceded in February 1861, and Lee, who had been ordered to report to Washington, arrived home at Arlington a month later. "I met Col. Robert E. Lee at Gen. Scott's office," one of his army friends wrote in his diary, March 5th. "He feels badly at the prospect." Probably all that Lee could tell his old friend was that if Virginia seceded he must follow her, and that all he could do was to await developments.

LEE RESIGNS FROM THE UNITED STATES ARMY. While Lee watched, helpless, events moved rapidly. Fort Sumter was bombarded in April, and in a few days Lee heard that his own beloved Virginia had seceded. Great as was his pride in the Union, he did not believe that it should be preserved by force; moreover, he felt his first allegiance was to his State. Though his career be sacrificed and the lives and property of his children endangered, he believed he must do his duty as he saw it.

Arlington blazed with lights Friday night, April 19, 1861, and was filled with relations and friends anxiously discussing the recent events. Finding it impossible to think about his problem amid the excitement, Colonel Lee went outside and paced back and forth under the trees while he pondered his future course. Still undecided, he returned to the house and went up to his bedroom. Downstairs, Mrs. Lee and the others waited anxiously. Overhead, they could hear Lee's footsteps as he paced the floor, stopping only when he knelt to pray. It was after midnight when he finally arrived at a decision and sat down to write his resignation from the United States Army. That done, he came down with it in his hand to where his wife was waiting. "Well, Mary," he said quietly, "the question is settled. Here is my letter of resignation, and a letter I have written to General Scott."

"Arlington House" as it appeared a few years before the Civil War. From a sketch by Benson J. Lossing.

A corner of the drawing room as restored about 1930.

THE LEES LEAVE ARLINGTON. Monday morning, Lee said goodbye to his family and left for Richmond. Before him were the long, hard years of a bitter war from which he would gain unfading glory. But never again would he be sheltered by the friendly roof of his old home at Arlington, and only once would he have a glimpse of it, and then from a passing train, several years after the war.

General Robert E. Lee in 1862. U. S. Army Signal Corps photograph.

In view of the strategic location of Arlington, Lee urged his wife to go to a place of safety, but no preparations had been made to leave when word reached Mrs. Lee, early in May, that the Federal forces were soon to move into Virginia. Then all was excitement as the family portraits were taken from their frames and, with the plate and the most valuable Washington relics, sent off for safekeeping. Curtains and carpets were packed away in the attic, books and engravings put in closets, and the china stored in boxes in the cellar. Most of the furniture had to be left behind, but this Mrs. Lee trusted she could recover later. When everything was in order, it was time to say farewell to the weeping servants, and to leave her home for what was to be the last time.

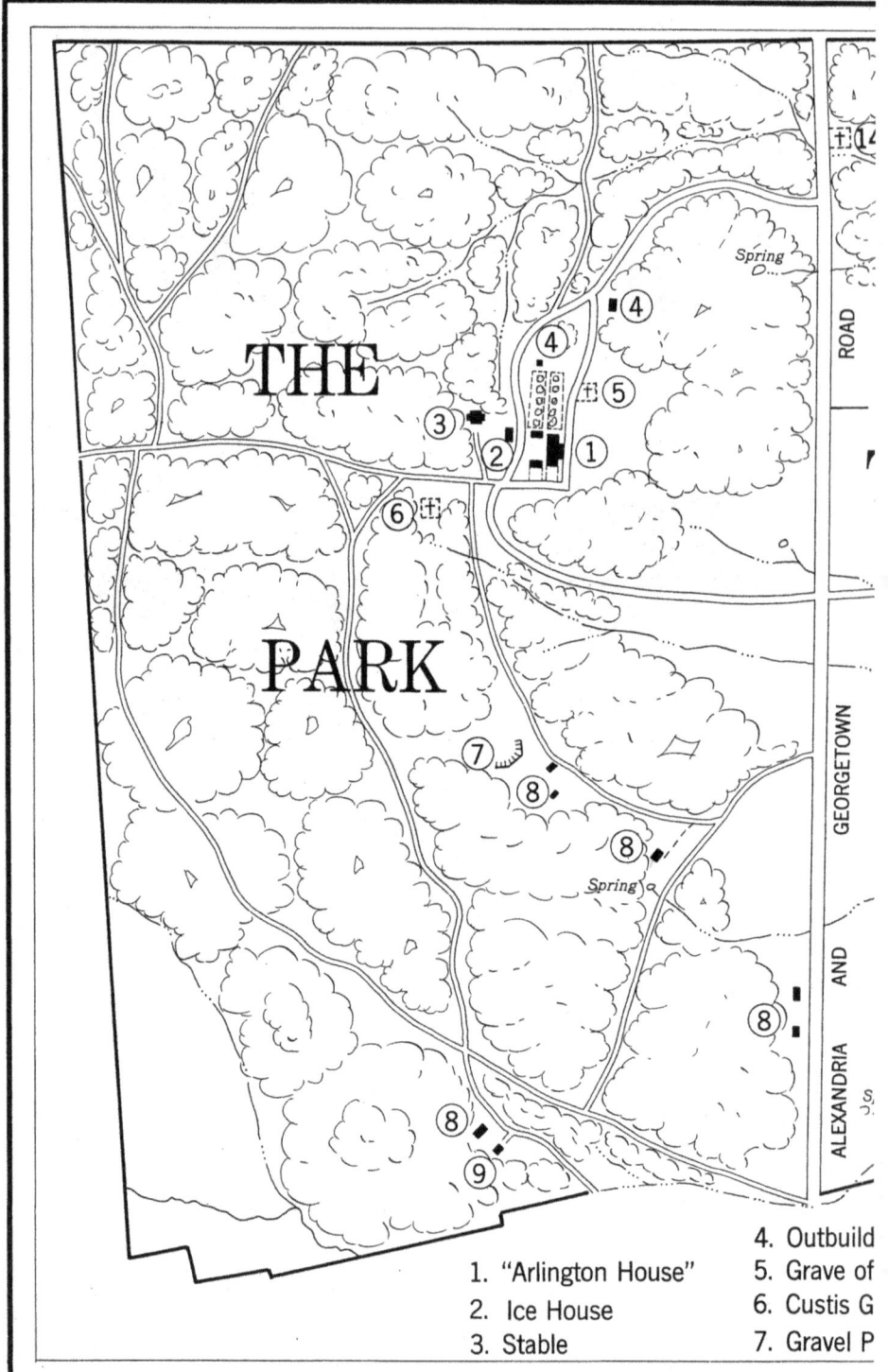

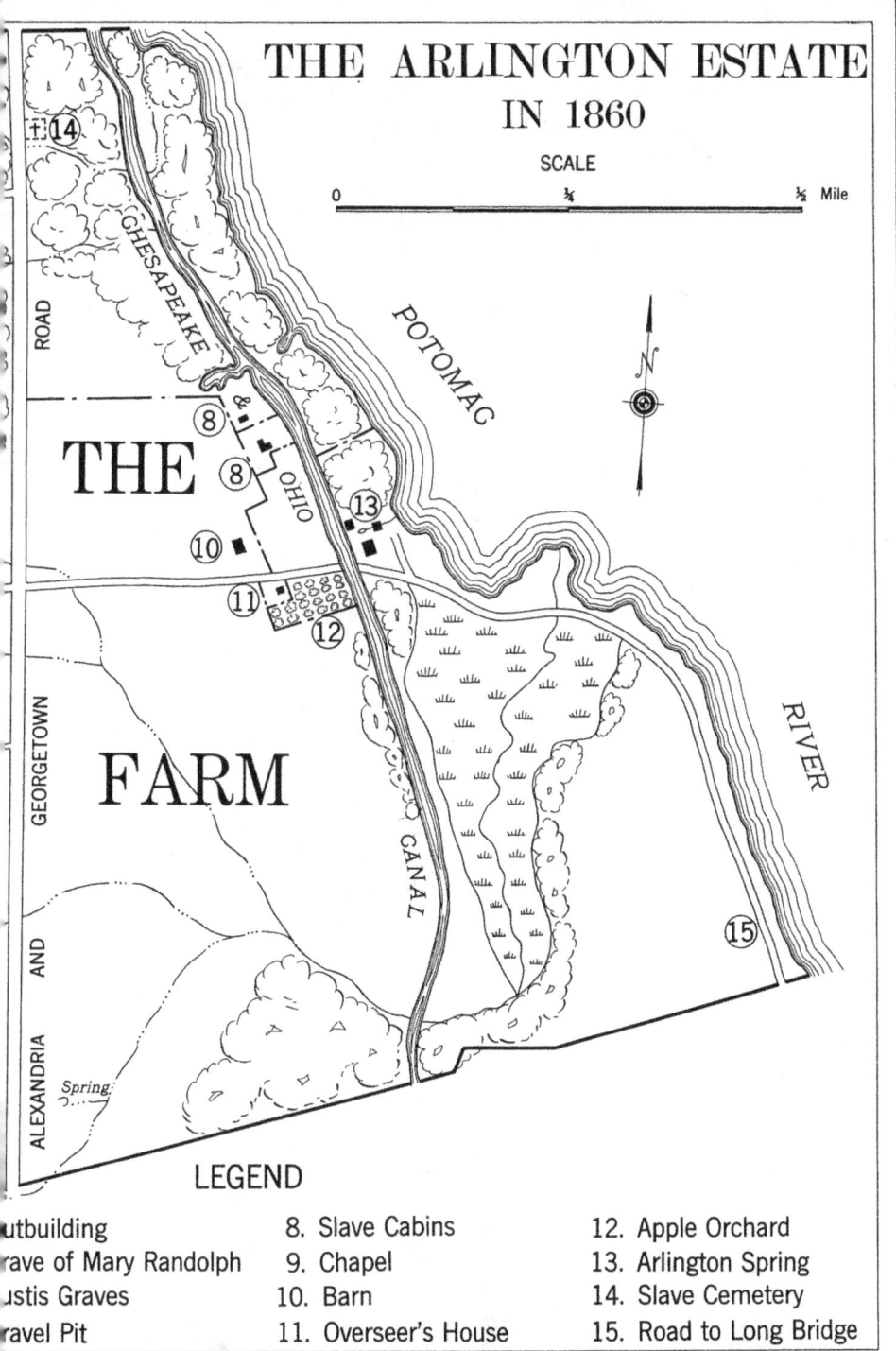

Arlington from 1861 to 1865

ARLINGTON OCCUPIED BY THE FEDERAL ARMY. Mrs. Lee had been gone only a few days when the Federal Army crossed the river and occupied the heights opposite the National Capital. Overnight, what had been a quiet country estate was transformed into a vast military encampment. New roads were cut through the woods and much of it felled to open fields of fire for the earthen forts being built a short distance west of the house. Guards were posted to protect the house, and when the commanding general learned that many articles nevertheless were being stolen, he sent the Washington relics, which had been stored in the cellar, to the Patent Office for safekeeping, and then established his headquarters inside the mansion. Inevitably, the estate suffered greatly, though strong efforts were made to prevent wanton destruction, particularly of the fine old trees.

LEE BECOMES THE HERO OF THE SOUTH. While Arlington was blighted by grim war, its former master was engaged in mobilizing the defenses of his native State. Before long he was military adviser to the President of the Confederacy, Jefferson Davis, and successively commander of the Army of Northern Virginia and general in chief of all the Confederate armies. The qualities developed by his years in the army and his home life were the same that now made him the military champion of the South and its greatest hero. His self-discipline rarely deserted him, and his deep religious beliefs gave him a humility and simplicity sufficient to withstand the greatest discouragements. Even though the odds were against him, his splendid presence on the field of battle and his kindliness and courtesy to all regardless of rank won him the devotion of his officers and men, while his brilliant military leadership gave hope and fighting spirit to the entire South. Always he was the knightly Christian gentleman, humane and magnanimous whether in victory or defeat.

East front of "Arlington House" in 1864. From the photograph by Brady in the National Archives.

Robert E. Lee in the full dress of a Confederate General. From the original photograph made in 1863 by Minnis and Cowell, Richmond.   U. S. Army Signal Corps photograph.

THE NATIONAL CEMETERY ESTABLISHED AT ARLINGTON, 1864. Early in 1862, the army moved away from Arlington for service in the field, but the mansion continued to be used as a headquarters by the generals commanding the troops and forts defending Washington. In 1864, the estate was sold for unpaid taxes and bought by the Government for its own use. In June of that year the first burials were made in 200 acres set aside as a national cemetery. Work was begun at once to restore the former natural beauty of the grounds, and by the end of the war almost all the scars caused by its military occupation had been erased. Only the long rows of white headboards gleaming among the trees and the desolate house now used only for the cemetery office bespoke the bitter strife that had wrought such a profound change at Arlington.

Arlington from 1865 to the Present

LEE'S INFLUENCE HELPS TO RESTORE THE SOUTH AFTER THE WAR. The splendid leadership which Lee had given his people during the war did not cease at Appomattox. As president of Washington College (afterwards Washington and Lee University), he devoted himself to restoring the South culturally, economically, and politically. Magnanimous in peace as in war, he urged his countrymen to forswear hatred and make the best of their situation. By his advice and example he did much to bring about the true restoration of the Union, not by force, but by the immeasurably stronger bonds of reconciliation and a common loyalty.

For a time General Lee hoped to regain possession of Arlington for his wife, but he died in 1870 without having recovered it. Mrs. Lee died 3 years later, and her son Custis then took legal action to obtain his inheritance. In 1882, the case was finally decided in his favor by the Supreme Court of the United States, but since thousands of soldiers had been buried at Arlington, Custis Lee accepted the offer of the Government to buy the property for one hundred and fifty thousand dollars.

ARLINGTON BECOMES FAMOUS AS THE FORMER HOME OF GENERAL LEE. Originally "Arlington House" had been famous for its associations with George Washington; but after the Civil War it became even more widely known as the former home of General Lee, and so it acquired its present name, "Lee Mansion." Though its rooms were empty, thousands from all over the country came to see it each year because of the universal admiration for its former master. It was in response to this sentiment that Representative Louis C. Cramton, of Michigan, sponsored the legislation passed by Congress in 1925 which authorized the restoration of the mansion as a national memorial.

RESTORATION OF THE LEE MANSION. The project of restoring and refurnishing the mansion was begun by the War Department in 1928.

Robert E. Lee in 1869 when President of Washington College, Lexington, Va. From the Brady photograph, U. S. Army Signal Corps.

Structural changes made since 1861 were removed and the house refurnished as nearly as possible as when occupied by the Lee and Custis families. The original furnishings having long since been scattered or lost, few could be returned to their old setting, but copies were made of furniture and portraits known to have been at Arlington and pieces appropriate to the period procured. By 1933, when the Lee Mansion was transferred to the National Park Service of the Department of the Interior, the major portion of the work was finished. The work of restoring the Lee Mansion to its original condition is a continuing process, however, as structural changes based on historical research are made and more of the original furnishings are identified and acquired.

27

Guide to the House and Grounds

THE OLD ARLINGTON ESTATE.   Arlington was but one of several estates totaling more than 15,000 acres owned by George Washington Parke Custis, father-in-law of General Lee. Since the former's income was largely derived from two large farms on the Pamunkey River in New Kent County, Va., he kept Arlington mainly as a gentleman's country estate after the English fashion. The greater part of Arlington was taken up by "the Park," a virgin woodland of ancient oaks and beautiful groves of walnut, chestnut, and elm trees, extending from the Georgetown and Alexandria Road at the foot of the hill clear to the western edge of the estate.

On the level land lying between the road and Potomac River was "the Farm," consisting of an orchard and several large cultivated fields and pastures. Here was grown most of the grain and vegetables required by the Arlington household and the large number of slaves, the surplus being sold in the Washington markets. In the southeast corner of the farm was the Arlington landing, where the barge which hauled produce to market was kept, as well as the schooner *Lady of the Lake,* used to carry goods to and from the distant farms. Here also docked the steamboats *Arlington Belle* and the *G. W. P. Custis,* which annually ferried thousands from the city to the famed Arlington Spring, for half a century a favorite picnic spot for Georgetown and Washington residents. For their convenience the hospitable owner erected pavilions for dining and dancing, requiring only that no liquor be used. Custis considered himself primarily a farmer, and spent most of each day riding or walking about the estate supervising the work being done. After he died in 1857 and the management of the estate was taken over by Col. Robert E. Lee, the area under cultivation was considerably enlarged.

Arlington originally had been part of a tract of 6,000 acres granted in 1669 by Governor William Berkeley of Virginia to a ship's captain, named Robert Howsing, in payment for transporting settlers to the colony. Howsing soon sold his grant to John Alexander, after whom Alexandria, Va., is named, reportedly for six hogsheads of tobacco. The land remained in the Alexander family until 1778, when John Parke Custis bought 1,100 acres from Gerard Alexander with the intention of establishing a family seat. He died, however, before he had done anything with the property, whereupon it passed to his son, George Washington Parke Custis, who developed it as described.

THE LEE MANSION.   For all its imposing appearance when seen at a distance, the real size of the mansion is not apparent until seen close at hand. The central part of the building is 2 stories high, 60 feet wide, and 40 feet deep. One-story wings, each 40 feet long and 25 feet wide, extend to the north and south, making the length of the entire building 140 feet. In the rear are still lower wings for service and a conservatory.

"Arlington House" from a sketch made before 1861, though not published until 1875.

Although the wings with their tall recessed windows and balustrade are quite pleasing, the magnificent portico is the salient architectural feature of the mansion, one of the earliest and best-known examples of Greek Doric porticos in America. This extends 25 feet from the front of the house and has 8 columns 23 feet high and somewhat over 5 feet thick at the base. Early authorities differ as to whether the portico was derived from the smaller, well-proportioned Greek temple at Athens known as the Theseum, or the larger, more imposing temple of Neptune at Paestum, Italy. There is no doubt, however, as to the effectiveness of the architectural style chosen, for no other would have had the strength and massiveness necessary to make the building impressive when viewed from across the river. Yet for all its simplicity and solidity, the proportions of the mansion are so refined as to make it an outstanding example of Greek Classic Revival architecture of the early nineteenth century.

The building is of the most solid construction throughout. All the walls and most of the foundations are of brick, as are the columns of the portico. All of the brickwork exposed to the weather is protected by hard stucco plaster scored with lines in imitation of cut stone. Joists, studs, and rafters are of hewn timber and are neatly mortised together or pinned with wooden pegs, scarcely any nails being used. Doors, cornices, and other woodwork are of pine. The main roof is supported by great barnlike trusses which span the entire width of the center section and originally was covered with wooden shingles, now replaced by slate. At one time the portico columns were painted to look like marble, but later were made white for better contrast with the warm buff or ochre color of the remainder of the house. Well constructed to begin with, the deterioration inevitable in any old building was entirely corrected when the War Department restored the building. Careful maintenance now assures a long and useful future for the Lee Mansion.

THE CONSERVATORY. Because flowers were important in the life of the Arlington household, it is most appropriate that present-day visitors enter the Lee Mansion through the conservatory. Both Mrs. Lee and her mother, Mrs. Custis, were devoted to their gardens and used flowers for decorations throughout the house. Called the "conservatory," or "greenhouse," and sometimes the "camellia house," by those who lived there, this was the room in which they grew their favorite flowers and plants during the winter months or started young ones for transplanting outdoors. The floor of the conservatory has been restored, but the door, woodwork, and most of the windows are original.

THE OFFICE AND STUDY. The management of a large estate like Arlington required an office where business could be transacted and records kept, and this long, narrow room was used as such by both Mr. Custis and Colonel Lee. Here the former worked on his literary efforts and carried on an extensive correspondence concerning agricultural matters and the life of General Washington. In his old age Mr. Custis also used it as

The conservatory.

MEASURED DRAWINGS OF THE MANSION

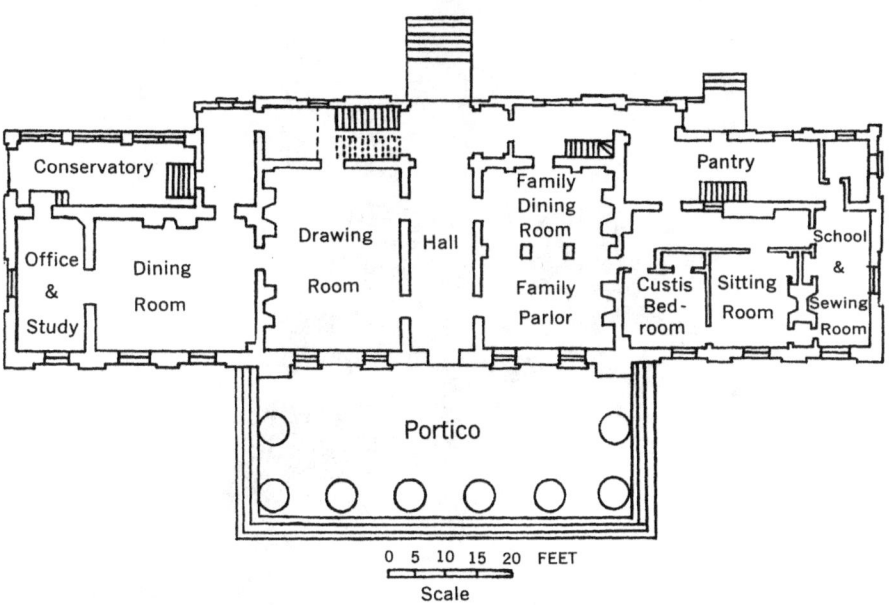

FIRST FLOOR PLAN

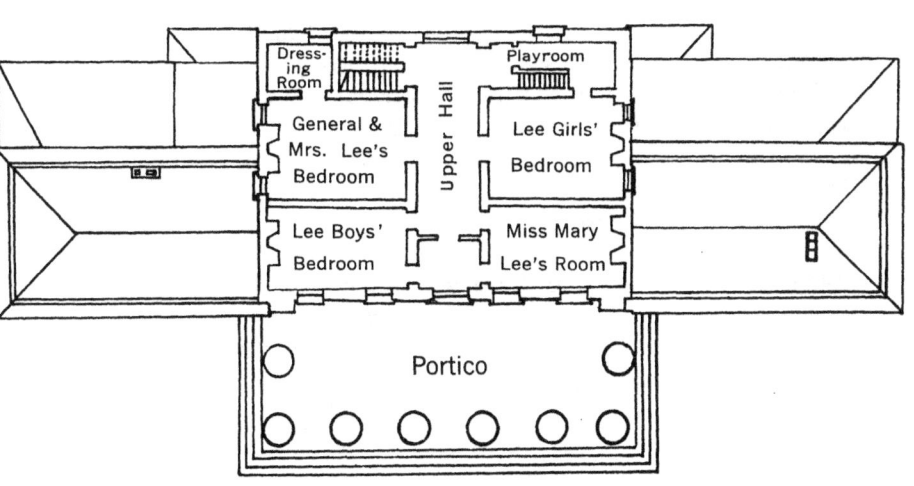

SECOND FLOOR PLAN

The office and study.

his "painting room," for in 1852 he wrote to a fellow artist: "I have an excellent studio fitted up in the South wing of the House, with a first rate light, . . . a stove & everything comfortable."

The desk in the corner was used by Lee during the years 1848 to 1852, while supervising the construction of Fort Carroll, near Baltimore, Md. Also of interest is his traveling chess set and the plain pine stand which Mrs. Lee gave to her personal maid, Selina Gray, whose descendants returned it to the house.

THE DINING ROOM. "The House will be a very showy handsome building when completed," wrote a lady visiting Arlington in 1804. "The room we were in was 24 feet square & 18 feet high," she continued. No doubt she was describing the present dining room, for here the Custises entertained their numerous guests before the large central section of the house was built. Later, Mr. Custis used it as a studio, and after his wife's death, in 1853, it became Mrs. Lee's "morning room," where she answered her mail and managed the affairs of her household. Here Mrs. Lee was engaged in copying a portrait of her infant grandson when, in May 1861, she was informed that the Federal Army was soon to occupy Arlington and that she must leave at once.

The dining room has been restored to its earliest use. Most of the woodwork and windows are original, while the molding, plaster, and the beautiful door to the study are entirely so. An interesting architectural feature is the great semicircular arch at the north end of the room, reminiscent of the villas Architect George Hadfield saw in Italy during the years he studied there.

THE DRAWING ROOM. The drawing room remained unfinished for many years, not even being plastered, probably because Mr. Custis lacked the necessary funds. During these years it was known as the "big room" and in it were stored old furniture and the finished canvasses of Mr. Custis. On rainy days the Lee children often used it as a playroom. When Colonel Lee went to Texas, in 1855, he left instructions for its "renovation"—plastering the walls, installing a crystal chandelier, and painting the walls and woodwork. He also ordered marble mantels for the fireplaces. Mrs. Lee supervised the progress of the work in her husband's absence, and the result must have been most pleasing, for a young lady who saw it in 1856 describes it as "a beautiful & noble drawing room, very handsomely furnished and hung too with paintings."

The most valuable paintings were taken away by Mrs. Lee in 1861, but copies have been made for the restoration of this room. The sofa is

The dining room.

original, as is the music rack near the piano. The woodwork and walls are finished off as Colonel Lee had them done in 1855.

THE HALL.   A long hall extending from the front to the back was a common feature of Virginia houses of the period, because of the cooling draft of air it provided during hot weather. For this reason it was usually furnished with sofas and chairs and used as a summer parlor. The Lees and Custises would sit and converse here on warm summer evenings, or perhaps read the latest English novel aloud to each other. "The puss has appropriated the sofa in the parlor to himself, while I occupy that in the hall," Mr. Custis observed humorously in a letter to his wife in 1831.

Characteristic of the Greek temples from which the Lee Mansion was adapted are the tall narrow doors at each end of the hall. The graceful round arches at the west end are typical of George Hadfield's architectural work. High on the walls at this end are the spirited hunting frescoes painted by Mr. Custis himself. Elk and deer horns represent the collection of antlers begun by him when a lad at Mount Vernon. Suspended from the ceiling in the middle of the hall is a replica of the famous Mount Vernon lantern, the original of which hung here for more than 50 years. On the walls are copies of portraits once at Arlington, including one of George Washington painted by Mr. Custis.

The drawing room.

THE FAMILY PARLOR. From an early date three arches have divided the large room north of the hall into a family parlor and a small dining room. Originally, there were doors and a fanlight in the center arch, while those on the outside were filled in with lath and plaster, probably to make the rooms easier to heat. The twin Carrara marble mantles are original, and are said to have been ordered by Mr. Custis from Italy.

The family parlor was the favorite gathering place of the Lees and Custises, who entertained most of their guests in it even after the drawing room was completed. Here the family passed the winter evenings reading or listening to Mr. Custis' interesting stories of his boyhood at Mount Vernon. Each Christmas it was the family custom to kindle the great yule log in the fireplace with the remains of that from the previous year. The wedding of Mary Custis and Robert E. Lee took place in this room, the bride and groom standing under the center arch during the ceremony. On the small table near the hall door is a framed letter which was discovered in the attic in 1926, written by Mary Lee Fitzhugh to George Washington Parke Custis before their marriage in 1804.

THE FAMILY DINING ROOM. Small and informal, the family dining room was used as such from the time the center section of the house was built until the Lees departed in 1861. Arlington was noted for its hospitality, and seldom was there a meal at which some guests were not present.

The family parlor.

When he was at home, it was Colonel Lee's custom to gather rosebuds in the garden each morning and place one beside the plate of each of his daughters, the youngest getting the smallest bud, and so on up to the eldest.

Over the mantel hangs a portrait of Mr. Custis, copied from the original in the Corcoran Gallery of Art, Washington, D. C. On the mantel is a statuette, "The Three Graces," said to have been imported from Italy by Mr. Custis about 1855. Among the dishes in the cupboard are two custard cups, a Wedgewood cream pitcher, and several other pieces which were originally at Arlington.

THE UPPER HALL. The simple staircase which ascends to the upper hall is typical of those in houses of classic revival style of architecture, since their temple prototypes had no second floor and hence no stairs. That the one in the Lee Mansion was carefully planned by the architect, however, is shown by the ingenious way in which one window serves to light the stair landing and the closet off it, as well as the hall below.

Like the one below, the upper hall was originally furnished with several long sofas for use as a sitting room during warm weather. At such times the lower part of the great window at the west end was opened wide in order to increase the movement of air.

The family dining room as seen from the family parlor. Mary Custis and Robert E. Lee stood under the middle arch during their marriage ceremony.

The family dining room.

THE LEE BEDROOM. This pleasant room was occupied by Mrs. Lee before and after her marriage. According to tradition, six of her seven children were born in the small dressing room on its west side. Mrs. Lee's toilet and serving case, resembling a miniature pulpit and bearing her initials "M. C. L.," sits on the bureau next to the door of the dressing room. On the mantel is an engraving of Mrs. Lee made at Arlington in 1858. This is the room in which Colonel Lee arrived at his decision to resign his commission in the United States Army.

THE BOYS' BEDROOM. This bedroom was occupied by the three Lee sons—Custis, Robert, and William Henry Fitzhugh, otherwise known as "Rooney." The floor, mantel, woodwork, and plaster in this room are original. The mahogany card table was at Arlington prior to 1861.

The main staircase.

The bedroom of Colonel and Mrs. Lee.

Next to the boys' room is a small chamber originally divided by a partition into dressing rooms for the adjoining bedrooms. In 1857, Mrs. Lee had the partition removed and a doorway made into the hall in order to provide more space for guests. Since the room was too small for a bed, a cot was set up whenever additional sleeping quarters were needed. The washstand and the Duncan Phyfe side chair are original Arlington pieces.

MISS MARY LEE'S ROOM. Miss Mary Lee, eldest of the Lee daughters, occupied this room from her earliest days. Occasionally, she shared it with one of her sisters, but more often with Martha Williams, known affectionately as Markie, a cousin of both Colonel and Mrs. Lee. Markie's mother died in 1843, and her father was killed 3 years later during the war with Mexico. Although Markie lived with her grandparents in Georgetown, she was at Arlington so much of the time as to be almost a member of the household, leading another guest to observe, in 1856, that "Markie's room commands a beautiful view of the river & of Washington." Markie and her father were both talented artists and several of their paintings embellished the house.

THE LEE GIRLS' BEDROOM. This large, sunny bedroom was occupied by Agnes, Annie, and Mildred Lee. Although it is not one of the original

Miss Mary Lee's room.

Arlington furnishings, the miniature mahogany bureau on the table against the west wall is noteworthy as having been owned by Anne Hill Carter Lee, mother of Robert E. Lee.

THE PLAYROOM. The small room next to the girls' bedroom served various purposes. When the girls were young it was their playroom. Later it was probably a dressing room, as indicated by the original shelves and coat pegs. It was also used by Annie Lee for the Sunday school she conducted for the children of the family servants. According to tradition, the miniature secretary at the back of the room was a childhood possession of Mr. Custis' sister, Nellie, who gave it to Mrs. Lee when she was little. Later it was given by Lee to his goddaughter, Nannie Randolph Heth.

The playroom.

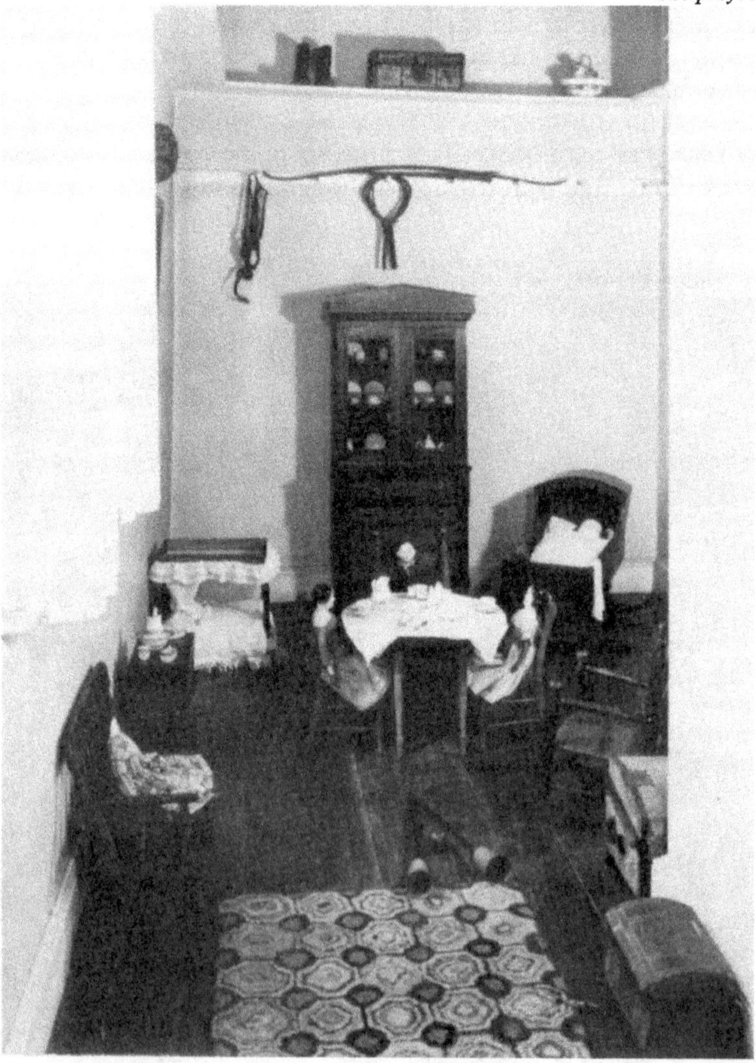

The Custis sitting room.

THE OUTER HALL. Visitors return to the first floor by the steep service stairway, intended primarily for the convenience of members of the family and servants. Like the second floor hall, the stairwell is painted as it was originally—a light peach. Beyond is the outer hall, originally the serving pantry for the nearby dining room. Here in its old location stands the walnut cupboard to which each night at bedtime Colonel Lee is said to have come for a glass of milk, brought there from the dairy room under the south wing.

THE CUSTIS ROOMS. An inner hall gave private access to the two small rooms in the north wing occupied by Mr. and Mrs. Custis in the years before the main part of the house was completed. Later they were probably used for guest rooms until such time as the size of the Lee family and the Custises' advancing years made it advisable for them to reoccupy their old suite. It is now restored as a bedroom and a sitting room. Under the bedroom window is a small mahogany candle stand once owned by Martha Washington and later part of the Arlington furnishings.

The wooden mantelpiece in the sitting room is the oldest one in the house, and its disproportionate size indicates that it was made for the large unused chimney breast in the inner hall.

The wooden mantelpiece in the Custis sitting room is the oldest in the house, dating from its earliest years.

THE SCHOOLROOM. This may have been Mrs. Lee's bedroom when she was a little girl and her parents occupied the adjoining rooms. After the main part of the house was built, it was used as a sewing room and a schoolroom for the Lee children and those of the house servants. The old terrestrial globe is one of the most interesting original objects in the mansion, having been found tucked away in the attic under the eaves by workmen repairing the roof some years ago. The small pine table on

The schoolroom.

The winter kitchen.

which it stands is also an original piece. Over the globe is a framed photograph of Commander Sidney Smith Lee, brother of Robert E. Lee.

THE WINTER KITCHEN. The huge fireplace in the winter kitchen under the north wing helped to warm the rooms above during the cold months of the year. The portion of the room beyond the chimney was used as a laundry.

THE WINE CELLAR. A quarterly return from one of Mr. Custis' estates, dated 1822, lists "2 hogsheads of cider, 2 barrels of A[pple] Brandy" as having been sent to Arlington. It was probably stored in this cool, dark room, together with the scuppernong wine made from grapes grown along the edge of the garden north of the mansion. Here also were kept the choicer vintages used for entertaining.

THE SERVANTS' QUARTERS. Two low buildings which harmonize architecturally with the main house form two sides of the court in the rear of the mansion. That on the north had a summer kitchen in the basement, its other rooms being occupied by the family servants. Perhaps because dampness made it unhealthy, the basement was filled in some years before 1861, but it is now restored to its original condition. The well between this building and the house is original, though the stone coping and roof are a restoration.

The corresponding building to the south was familiarly known as "Selina's House," because its western end was occupied by Mrs. Lee's personal maid, Selina Gray, and her family. The middle room was the smokehouse, and on the east end was the storeroom where nonperishable household provisions were kept. The small panels over the doors were originally painted by Mr. Custis, the one in the center depicting Gen-

The north servants' quarters and the well.

The Lee Mansion as seen from the west.

eral Washington's war horse and the others, American eagles. Old photographs show similar panels decorating the north quarters, but these have long since weathered away.

THE GARDENS. The flower garden originally occupied the large level plot south of the mansion. Gravel paths divided the area into flower beds, and in the center stood a wooden arbor almost covered with yellow jasmine and honeysuckle. Mr. Custis had laid out the garden in his early years, but the responsibility for its care was soon assumed by Mrs. Custis, who loved flowers. Mrs. Lee acquired her mother's interest in gardening and had her own flower beds, while each of her daughters, as soon as they were old enough, were given small plots in which to grow their favorite blooms. Roses of different species predominated, the Cherokee being a favorite of Mrs. Custis', but there were also many other kinds of flowers and plants. It was the family custom to exchange seeds and plants with friends and relatives, thus adding to the variety of lovely blooms at Arlington.

North of the mansion, on the site of the present rose garden, was the "kitchen garden" where the vegetables used by the household were grown. Here were strawberry and asparagus beds, tomato vines and many other vegetables, as well as a number of fruit trees. Grapevines said to have been planted by Mrs. Lee, and which are still bearing, grow at its north and east sides. The building at the north end is not an original structure, though it stands on the site of an earlier outbuilding.

THE GRAVE OF MARY RANDOLPH. The grave of Mary Randolph, believed to have been Mrs. Lee's godmother, is a short distance from the northeast corner of the mansion, down the Custis walk which here approximates the course of the old carriage driveway. Mrs. Randolph was related to both the Custises and the Lees and was well known in the early part of the nineteenth century as the author of an extremely popular cookbook, *The Virginia Housewife*. She and her husband, David Meade Randolph, were often at Arlington, the latter being the inventor of a special waterproof stucco used on part of the exterior of the mansion. Mrs. Randolph died in 1828 and was the first person buried at Arlington. The ivy growing on the brick enclosure about her tomb is said to have been planted by Mr. and Mrs. Custis.

THE CUSTIS GRAVES. A few hundred yards southwest of the mansion, Doubleday Walk passes a small plot enclosed by an iron fence. Here beneath the beautiful trees in the spot selected by Mrs. Lee are the graves of her mother and father. Colonel Lee ordered the marble monuments from New York, specifying that a wreath of lilies of the valley and heartsease should be carved on the one for Mrs. Custis' grave. He also supervised their erection.

Visitor Service and Facilities

Lee Mansion National Memorial is located in Arlington National Cemetery and is reached by way of Arlington Memorial Bridge. Bus service is available via Arlington Memorial Bridge to the main gate of the cemetery. Automobiles use the same approach and may be parked near the mansion. Visiting hours, October through March, are from 9:30 a. m. to 4:30 p. m.; April through September, 9:30 a. m. to 6 p. m. There is a small admission charge, which is waived for children and educational groups.

Administration

Lee Mansion National Memorial is administered by the National Capital Parks of the National Park Service, United States Department of the Interior. Other national memorials administered by the National Capital Parks are: The Lincoln Memorial, the Thomas Jefferson Memorial, the Washington Monument, the Lincoln Museum, and the House Where Lincoln Died. Communications should be addressed to the Superintendent, National Capital Parks, Washington 25, D. C.

www.ingramcontent.com/pod-product-compliance
Lightning Source LLC
Chambersburg PA
CBHW031433040426
42444CB00006B/788